Keto Ninja Foodi

Simple and Delicious Low Carb High Fat Ketogenic Recipes for a Healthy Keto Lifestyle (Burn Fat, Balance Hormones and Reverse Disease)

Jane Lee

© Copyright 2018 Jane Lee- All Rights Reserved.

In no way is it legal to reproduce, duplicate, or transmit any part of this document by either electronic means or in printed format. Recording of this publication is strictly prohibited, and any storage of this material is not allowed unless with written permission from the publisher. All rights reserved.

The information provided herein is stated to be truthful and consistent, in that any liability, regarding inattention or otherwise, by any usage or abuse of any policies, processes, or directions contained within is the solitary and complete responsibility of the recipient reader. Under no circumstances will any legal liability or blame be held against the publisher for any reparation, damages, or monetary loss due to the information herein, either directly or indirectly.
Respective authors own all copyrights not held by the publisher.

Legal Notice:
This book is copyright protected. This is only for personal use. You cannot amend, distribute, sell, use, quote or paraphrase any part of the content within this book without the consent of the author or copyright owner. Legal action will be pursued if this is breached.

Disclaimer Notice:
Please note the information contained within this document is for educational and entertainment purposes only. Every attempt has been made to provide accurate, up-to-date and reliable, complete information. No warranties of any kind are expressed or implied. Readers acknowledge that the author is not engaging in the rendering of legal, financial, medical or professional advice.

By reading this document, the reader agrees that under no circumstances are we responsible for any losses, direct or indirect, which are incurred as a result of the use of information contained within this document, including, but not limited to, errors, omissions, or inaccuracies.

Table of contents

Chapter 1: Understanding the Keto Diet 9

The History of Keto 9

The Process of Ketosis 9

How to Reach 'Ketosis'? 9

- Restriction of carbs: 9
- Restriction of Proteins: 9
- Consume Enough Fat: 10
- Try Avoiding snacking: 10
- Intermittent Fasting: 10
- Regular Exercising: 10
- Sufficient Sleep: 11

Advantages of Keto Diet 11

- Weight Loss: 11
- Controlled Appetite: 11
- Surplus Energy and Mental Boosting: 12
- Reversing Type-2 Diabetes & Controlling Blood Sugar: 12
- Improvement in Health Markers: 12
- Stomach Improvement: 12
- Improvement in Physical Strength: 13
- Epilepsy Treatment: 13
- Additional Benefits: 13

Chapter-2: The Reinvention of the Cooking Pot 14

What is the Ninja Foodi? 14

    The Main Functions: 14

    What is the TenderCrisp™ Technology? 14

    Benefits of the Ninja Foodi 15

    How to use the Ninja Foodi? 16

Chapter 3: Food to Eat and Food to Avoid *17*

    Foods which are recommended 17

    Foods which are not recommended 17

Chapter-4: Tips *18*

    Tips for Keto Diet: 18

    Tips for Ninja Foodi: 18

Chapter-5: Breakfast Recipes *19*

    Morning Hash 19

    Broccoli Cheese Scrambled Eggs 20

    Spinach Quiche 21

    Tofu with Mushrooms 22

    Bacon Veggies Combo 23

    Onion Tofu Scramble 24

    Pepperoni Omelet 25

    Ham Spinach Ballet 26

    Sausage Solo 27

Bacon Bok Choy Samba 28

Chapter 6: Snacks and Appetizers Recipes *29*

   Eggs Stuffed with Avocado & Watercress 29

   Cheese Casserole 30

   Avocado Chips 31

   Scallion Cake 32

   Mixed Nuts 34

   Asparagus Bites 35

   Broccoli Pops 36

   Zucchini Cream Cheese Fries 37

Chapter 7: Vegetarian Recipes *38*

   Mediterranean Spinach with Cheese 38

   Cheesy Veggies 39

   Stunning Broccoli Florets 40

   Cauliflower Mash 41

   Nutty Brussels Sprouts 42

   Luncheon Green Beans 43

   Vegetable Dinner Casserole 44

   Cheesy Cauliflower 45

Chapter 8: Fish and Seafood Recipes *46*

Salmon Stew 46

Paprika Shrimp 47

Ketogenic Butter Fish 48

Shrimp Magic 49

Sweet and Sour Fish 50

Buttered Scallops 51

Buffalo Fish 52

Cod: Battle of Herbs 53

Chapter 9: Poultry Recipes *54*

Chicken Ropa Vieja 55

Ham Stuffed Turkey Rolls 57

Stuffed Whole Chicken 58

Creamy Turkey Breast 59

Caprese Hasselback Chicken 60

Mediterranean Turkey Cutlets 61

Keto Garlic Turkey Breasts 62

Chili Lime Chicken 63

Chapter 10: Beef, Pork and Lamb Recipes *64*

Garlic Creamy Beef Steak 64

Ketogenic Beef Sirloin Steak 65

Bacon Swiss Pork Chops 66

Crock Pot Beef Fajitas 67

Jamaican Jerk Pork Roast 68

Crispy Pork Carnitas 69

Mexican Taco Casserole 70

Mustard Pork Chops 71

Zesty Lamb Chops 72

Lamb Roast 73

Keto Lamb Minced Meat 74

Greek Lamb Gyros 75

Indian Beef 76

Classical Steak Meal 78

Meat Loaf 80

Chapter 11: Desserts Recipes *82*

Chocolate Peanut Butter Cups 82

Crème Brûlée 83

Flourless Chocolate Brownies 84

Cream Crepes 85

Nut Porridge 86

Lemon Mousse 87

Chocolate Cheese Cake 88

Vanilla Yogurt 89

Coffee Custard 90

Fudge Divine... 91

Conclusion.. *92*

Chapter 1: Understanding the Keto Diet

The History of Keto

It was discovered by Roller Turner in the year 1921 that ketone structures like acetone, β-hydroxybutyrate and acetoacetate are formed inside the liver after consuming a low carbohydrate and high fat content diet. This major breakthrough was the result of the research of Roller Turner on how diabetes and diet is interring related to each other. The ketogenic diet was the output of Dr. Russel Wilder upon further researching on the findings of Roller Turner. The keto diet was then used in 1921 on individuals having epilepsy to infer its effects on them and surprisingly the results were promising.

The Process of Ketosis

The body when starts using fats (by burning them) for its working instead of blood glucose (sugar bodies) is known to be in the process of ketosis. The process of ketosis leads to the production of ketones in the body. The kept diet is based on the principle of ketosis and it offers various advantages to its followers. These advantages (both financial and health) will be further explained in the coming portions of this book.

How to Reach 'Ketosis'?

"Reaching" ketosis has many aspects to it and there are various thigs which play a significant role in increasing and enhancing your body ketone content. These factors are explained elbow in the orders of its significance and effectiveness from top to bottom:

Restriction of carbs:

You can improve your ketone levels significantly by reducing your carb intake to 20g per day (digestible) or even lower than this. It is very important to understand that fiber is a very important nutrient and its consumption shouldn't be lowered than the needs of your body. The most important thing to understand about ketosis is that ketosis is an output of a lower carb consumption and the rest of the steps you take to enhance your ketosis simply guarantees the success of the process of ketosis over a long-time span.

Restriction of Proteins:

For achieving a perfect ketosis apart from low carbs, a mild intake of proteins also plays an important role. Proteins should be taken in a mild quantity as their excess results into their transition into blood glucose and it can have a negative impact on your ketone levels.

Consume Enough Fat:

One thing should be very clear, fasting to achieve ketosis and following a keto diet for reaching ketosis are two exclusive things. The reason is that fasting for a longer time is near to impossible and above all it has a very negative impact on your health. While on the other hand the keto diet can be conveniently followed by anybody for an entire life span. The harmful aspects of fasting for long time includes being tired, giving up on fasting itself and hunger. Contrary to this, keto diet offers many benefits to its followers and can be adapted as a life style. Fat is a very important nutrient of or diet and if you have constant hunger, go for some extra fat in your diet in the form of more quantity of olive oil etc.

Try Avoiding snacking:

While following keto, don't consume additional snacks if you are not that much hungry. Consuming more food than your body needs not only slows down the pace of ketosis but also creates hindrances in losing weight. If you are unable to control your huger, you can snack with a keto meal but not anything apart from it.

Intermittent Fasting:

You can even fast on the keto diet, but it's not entirely fasting, it's more of an intermittent fasting. If you want to have a perfect intermittent fasting, just eat for 8 hours in the day and fast for the rest of the remaining 16 hours. The intermittent fasting plays an important role in increasing the ketosis levels, initiating weight loss and reversing type-2 diabetes.

Regular Exercising:

Exercising or working out regularly while consuming a low carb diet also plays an assistive role in enhancing the ketosis process of your body. Apart from this, it has a very low-level impact on reversing type-2 diabetes and aiding in weight loss. It's not mandatory to work out for improving ketosis, it simply supports in incrementing the ketosis process.

Sufficient Sleep:

A perfect average sleep time is considered to be between 7 to 8 hours per night. For improving your ketosis, have sound sleep and reduce your stress as much as you can. Sleep deprivation and stress hormones are responsible for incrementing blood sugar levels, reducing the process of ketosis and having a slight impact in hindering weight loss too.

In conclusion, for reaching perfect ketosis, reduce your carbohydrates intake. Reduce the carb content to somewhere near to 20 carbohydrates every day. This is the most significant aspect for initiating and establishing the process of ketosis. For achieving a perfect ketosis, follow the above steps in their ascending order from the top.

Advantages of Keto Diet

There are vast similarities between the benefits of keto diet and other low carb and high fats, but the keto diet is considered to be far more effective and powerful in its working and advantages. The keto diet provides you with super-charged powers as compared to other low carb diets and provides you with a long list of benefits which have long lasting effects on your health and growth. A few of these advantages are as follows:

Weight Loss:

The effectiveness of keto diet in weight loss is easy to comprehend from the usage of fats as the main energy source by the body for its working. As soon as the glucose levels fall, weigh loss initiates. This condition enables an ideal environment for drastic weight loss without having an urge to eat or in simpler words, without hunger. There are more than 20 various modern scientific researches that proves that the keto des is the most effective diet plan in weight loss as compared to its competitors.

Controlled Appetite:

When on keto diet, you will feel less urge to eat or lower hunger because when fats are burnt for energy purposes, they are available in abundance in your body and you don't feel the urge to eat more for the working of your body. The reduced hunger aids in weight loss, assist you during intermittent fasting and also enhances the reversal of type-2 diabetes. The controlled appetite is very feasible in terms of finance as the expenditure on food lowers down drastically.

In terms of health, having controlled appetite or lower urge to eat food lowers down both food and sugar addiction as well as avoiding food related disorders like bulimia etc. being satisfied s the basic reason for being successful in the keto plan. Your food acts more as a friend and energy stimulator rather than act as an enemy and deteriorate your health.

Surplus Energy and Mental Boosting:

The steady flow of energy to the brain in form of ketones is provided by the process of 'ketosis' and its lets you either lower down or entirely avoid blood sugar swings. This aids a lot in clearing brain fog and increasing your concentration too. The keto diet is very famous for its tremendous benefits on mental focus and health. One can easily experience these critical advantages during ketosis. The process of ketosis lets the human brain have surplus and continuous energy in the form of ketones which results in improved focus and mental health.

Reversing Type-2 Diabetes & Controlling Blood Sugar:

It is understood by the process of ketosis that the keto diet reduces the number of blood sugar levels and reduces the harmful impacts of incremented insulin levels. Apart from merely reversing type-2 diabetes, the keto diet assists you as much as it can to avoid the risk of catching the disease in the first place and it does so by reversing pre-diabetic conditions.

Improvement in Health Markers:

The lower consumption of carbohydrates ensures improvement in important health markers like glucose levels, blood pressure levels and cholesterol levels (triglycerides and HDL). These health markers are directly related with metabolic syndrome, weight improvements, reversal of type-2 diabetes and waist circumference etc.

Stomach Improvement:

The keto diet is very beneficial for stomach health. It is effective in reducing both cramps and pains as well as little or no gas at all inside your stomach. You can experience this merely after 2-3 days of following of the plan. The cause for bloating or gas is that FODMAP (having high carbs) ferment inside the small intestine. The gut walls don't absorb them properly and this leads to the fluid stuck inside the intestine leading to diarrhea. The keto diet is very low in its FODMAP content and rather behaves like an anti IBS approach. The gradual removal of carbohydrates from your diet has a very good effect on your digestive system.

Improvement in Physical Strength:

The keto diet enhances both physical endurance and strength because it provides regular and continuous energy to the body in the shape of fats. The energy credited by carbs (glycogens) merely lasts for a few hours for high level workouts. Contrary to them, the energy due to ketones last for more than weeks and in cases months in the body and improves the physical efficiency of the body befittingly.

Epilepsy Treatment:

The keto diet has been in use to treat epilepsy since the 1920s. In the early days it was just used in children but ow its being tested on adults too and the results are promising. The keto diet lowers the medication intake of the patients or in some cases they might cease to use any medication at all without having the fear of anymore seizures. This reduces drug intake and improves mental efficiency too. Epilepsy is controlled with the keto diet with very little or no medication at all. This lets the patients avoid drug related complications like concentration loss, drowsiness etc.

Additional Benefits:

There is a lot more to the keto diet than the above mentioned prominent benefits. There are various advantages of the keto diet which can be game changer or life saving for many people across the globe. Lower consumption of carbohydrates benefits you with many things like migraine control, lesser acne issues, blood pressure controlling and even aids in certain mental health complications. Some of the additional benefits of the keto diet are as follows:

- Lesser Acne
- Reversing PCOS
- Lesser Heartburn
- Fewer Migraine Attacks
- Treatment of Brain Cancer
- Lesser Sugar Cravings
- Alzheimer treatment
- BP level controlling

Chapter-2: The Reinvention of the Cooking Pot

What is the Ninja Foodi?

Ninja®, is a very innovative manufacturer in various household appliances has made a major breakthrough in cooking with the Ninja® Foodi™ which is basically a pressure cooker that crisps like an air fryer. It's a combo of both pressure cooking and air frying which is being offered by a single appliance for the first time. It uses the TenderCrisp™ technology for its working (explained in coming portions). It not only cooks and tenders your food, but its significant crisping lid lets you air fry, broil, roast/bake your food with the final food to be juicy with an outer crisp.

The Main Functions:

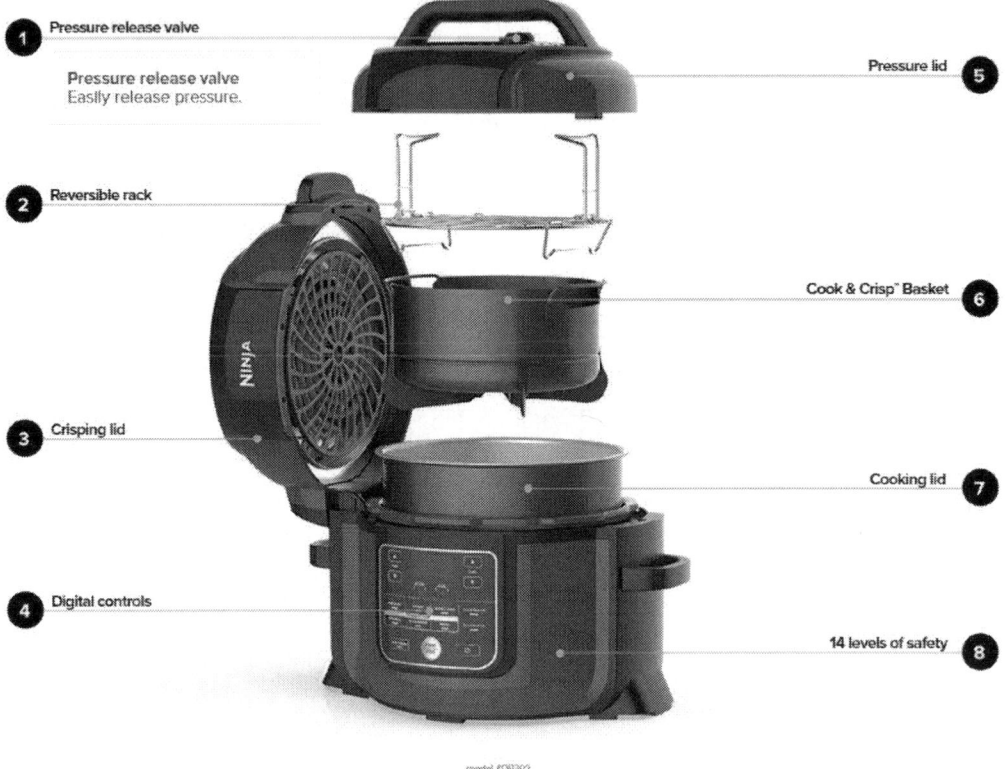

What is the TenderCrisp™ Technology?

Cooking tougher ingredients or meats with pressure cooking makes them into a much tender and delicious food. On the other hand, air frying makes our food crispier and have a tasty crust in it. The combo of both air frying and pressure cooking is the basic working principle of Ninja Foodi and is called the TenderCrisp Technology. It creates a perfect tender and juicy food which is crispy on its outer surface. The cooking procedures initiates with pressure cooking, followed by a customized air frying standard to achieve the crispiness of your choice.

TenderCrisp™ Technology utilizes steam (super-heated) to infuse both flavor and moisture faster into the food cooked with pressure cooking. Afterwards the crisping lid blows down hot air to every corner of your food and makes it crispier and finishes it with a certain golden color which can't be achieved by any other cooking appliance.

Benefits of the Ninja Foodi

1. The Ninja Foodi is very convenient in operation. It resembles the Instant Pot and similar electric pressure cooking appliance in its operation.
2. Its sturdy and perfectly manufactured.
3. The display window is very convenient, and it shows all the necessary information like time left for cooking, when to close the lid, what exactly is happening inside the pot and much more than this. To show information about pressure, the blue lights rotate in a square which is shown on the display board during its pressurization period and the lights go out when the required pressure is achieved.
4. The user manual and instructions inside it are very understandable and are written very clearly removing any ambiguities.
5. There is a cookbook along with the unit and in addition to it, for cooking generally cooked food items, there is a special cheat sheet.
6. The unit is provided with a reversible rack both for lower and higher positions apart from a Cook & Crisp basket.
7. The coating on the pot is well established and is made of ceramic of such a good quality that it can be resembled to a proper stainless-steel pot.
8. Air frying with the Ninja Foodi is nearly perfect for making crispy foods.
9. As soon as the air frying time is up, the unit automatically stops the air frying and doesn't require your manual touch to stop.
10. The pot of the Foodi is comparatively shorter and wider in width than the Instant Pot. It is very great for prepping desserts like crème brulee etc. The reason is that there is extra space for perfect browning of the food and it can fit nearly 4 custard cups inside it without stacking them on top of each other.

How to use the Ninja Foodi?

The food with the Ninja Foodi is the best both a pressure cooker and air fryer can give you, but this time it's going to be in a single pot. You can transform frozen foods into the most delicious crispy meals for yourself. You can prepare wholesome food with multi-texture 360 meals by preparing vegetables, grains and proteins in a single go. The Ninja Foodi can be used as the following appliances as per our needs:

1. Air Fryer
2. Pressure Cooker
3. Slow Cooker
4. Steamer
5. Multi Cooker
6. Broiler
7. Oven for baking/roasting
8. Food Dehydrator (only in limited editions)
9. Stovetop for sautéing/searing

Chapter3: Food to Eat and Food to Avoid

Foods which are recommended

The following foods are considered to be the most effective for the keto diet plan. They are considerably low on carbs. These include:

1. Leafy green veggies like kale and spinach etc.
2. Above ground veggies like cauliflower, broccoli and zucchini etc.
3. Avocados
4. Fruits like lemon juice, lime juice, prickly pears, grapefruit, coconut, rhubarb, star fruit and casaba melon etc.
5. Seeds and nuts like almonds, pumpkin seeds, sunflower seeds and pistachios etc.
6. Berries like blackberries, raspberries and other impact berries which are low glycemic in nature.
7. Fats like MCT oil, coconut oil, red palm oil and olive oil etc.
8. Sweeteners like monk fruit, erythritol, stevia and other sweeteners which are low carb in nature.
9. Dairy products like Greek yogurt, heavy whipping cream, cottage cheese, cream cheese, mascarpone, Monterey jack, parmesan cheese, mayo and mayonnaise alternatives having dairy, butter etc.

Foods which are not recommended

The following categories of foods are not allowed while following the keto diet plan. These foods are high in their carb content and can have a negative effect on your plan:

1. Legumes like peas, lentils and black beans etc.
2. Grains like cereals, rice, wheat and corn rice, rye, oats, quinoa, barley, millet, bulgur, amaranth etc.
3. Sugar rich foods like honey, cane sugar, Splenda, saccharin, agave nectar, aspartame and maple syrup etc.
4. Tubers like yams and potatoes etc.
5. Fruits like oranges, bananas and apples etc.

Chapter-4: Tips

Tips for Keto Diet:
- Exercising Regularly
- Fasting Fitfully
- Reducing Protein Consumption
- Having Proper Sleep Cycle
- Frequent Usage of MCT Oils
- Relieving Stress

Tips for Ninja Foodi:
- The device is heavy and larger in, so it requires a larger space in your kitchen.
- Cooking with the Foodi under a cabinet is very hard. The air fryer lid (crisping lid) is attached and non-removable, rather its hinge. For using the pressure cooker lid, the crisping lid requires space for opening.
- You need to use the Foodi near a power outlet as the electrical chord with the Foodi is just 33" in length. It is also mentioned in the instructions manual to avoid using any type of extension cord for safety measures.
- The Foodi has a different pressure releasing valve than the Instant Pot valve. It is hard to operate and short, thus making it difficult not to get burnt by the steam released.
- You will have to keep the Foodi aside from cabinets and walls as the hot air is released from the back side as it functions as an Air Fryer.
- Accessories which can be generally be compatible with the pressure cookers of 6 quarts will be comparatively much taller to be used with the Foodi.
- The warning sound (beep) after your food is prepared is not much louder and can't be adjusted (increased or decreased).

Chapter-5: Breakfast Recipes
Morning Hash

Preparation Time: 10 minutes
Cooking Time: 20 minutes
Servings: 2
Ingredients:

- 1 tablespoon unsalted butter
- ½ teaspoon dried thyme, crushed
- ½ cup cauliflower florets, boiled and chopped
- ½ small onion, chopped
- ½ cup water
- Salt and black pepper, to taste
- ½ pound turkey meat, chopped
- ¼ cup heavy cream

Method:

1. Press "Sauté" on Ninja Foodi and add butter and onions.
2. Sauté for about 3 minutes and add chopped cauliflowers.
3. Sauté for about 2 minutes and add turkey and water.
4. Close the lid and set the Ninja Foodi to "High Pressure" for about 10 minutes.
5. Release the pressure quickly and open the lid.
6. Press "Broil" and add heavy cream.
7. Cook for about 2 minutes and dish out to serve.

Nutritional Value:

- Calories 151
- Total Fat 11.6 g
- Saturated Fat 4.6 g
- Cholesterol 335 mg
- Total Carbs 0.7 g
- Sugar 0.7 g
- Sodium 144 mg
- Potassium 119 mg
- Protein 11.1 g

Broccoli Cheese Scrambled Eggs

Preparation Time: 5 minutes
Cooking Time: 8 minutes
Servings: 6
Ingredients:
- 2 tablespoons butter
- 12 ounces broccoli florets
- Salt and black pepper, to taste
- ¼ cup water
- ¾ cup cheddar cheese, shredded
- 8 eggs
- 2 tablespoons milk

Method:
1. Press "Sauté" on Ninja Foodi and add butter and broccoli in the pot.
2. Sauté for about 3 minutes and add water, salt and black pepper.
3. Close the lid and set the Ninja Foodi to "High Pressure" for about 7 minutes.
4. Release the pressure quickly and open the lid.
5. Press "Sauté" and whisk in eggs, milk salt and pepper.
6. Sauté for about 2 minutes and add cheese.
7. Press "Air Crisp" at 320 degrees F and cook for 2 more minutes.
8. Dish out and serve.

Nutritional Value:
- Calories 197
- Total Fat 14.6 g
- Saturated Fat 7.3 g
- Cholesterol 244 mg
- Total Carbs 4.7 g
- Sugar 1.7 g
- Fiber 1.5 g
- Sodium 219 mg
- Potassium 276 mg
- Protein 12.7 g

Spinach Quiche

Preparation Time: 10 minutes
Cooking Time: 33 minutes
Servings: 6
Ingredients:
- 1 tablespoon butter, melted
- 1 (10-ounce) package frozen spinach, thawed
- 5 organic eggs, beaten
- Salt and black pepper, to taste
- 3 cups Monterey Jack cheese, shredded

Method:
1. Press "Sauté" on Ninja Foodi and add butter and spinach.
2. Sauté for about 3 minutes and dish out in a bowl.
3. Add eggs, Monterey Jack cheese, salt and black pepper to a bowl and transfer into greased molds.
4. Place the molds inside the pot of Ninja Foodi and press "Bake/Roast".
5. Set the timer to 30 minutes at 360 degrees F and press "Start".
6. Remove from the Ninja Foodi after 30 minutes and cut into equal sized wedges to serve.

Nutritional Value:
- Calories 349
- Total Fat 27.8 g
- Saturated Fat 14.8 g
- Cholesterol 229 mg
- Total Carbs 3.2 g
- Sugar 1.3 g
- Fiber 1.3 g
- Sodium 532 mg
- Potassium 466 mg
- Protein 23 g

Tofu with Mushrooms

Preparation Time: 10 minutes
Cooking Time: 10 minutes
Servings: 6
Ingredients:
- 8 tablespoons Parmesan cheese, shredded
- 2 cups fresh mushrooms, finely chopped
- 2 blocks tofu, pressed and cubed into 1-inch pieces
- Salt and black pepper, to taste
- 8 tablespoons butter

Method:
1. Mix together tofu, salt and black pepper in a bowl.
2. Press "Sauté" on Ninja Foodi and add butter and seasoned tofu.
3. Sauté for about 5 minutes and add mushrooms and Parmesan cheese.
4. Sauté for about 3 minutes and press "Air Crisp".
5. Cook for about 2 minutes at 350 degrees F and dish out in a serving plate.

Nutritional Value:
- Calories 211
- Total Fat 18.5 g
- Saturated Fat 11.5 g
- Cholesterol 51 mg
- Total Carbs 2 g
- Sugar 0.5 g
- Fiber 0.4 g
- Sodium 346 mg
- Potassium 93 mg
- Protein 11.5 g

Bacon Veggies Combo

Preparation Time: 5 minutes
Cooking Time: 25 minutes
Servings: 4
Ingredients:
- 1 green bell pepper, seeded and chopped
- 4 bacon slices
- ½ cup Parmesan Cheese
- 1 tablespoon avocado mayonnaise
- 2 scallions, chopped

Method:
1. Arrange bacon slices in the pot of Ninja Foodi and top with avocado mayonnaise, bell peppers, scallions and Parmesan Cheese.
2. Press "Bake/Roast" and set the timer to 25 minutes at 365 degrees F.
3. Remove from the Ninja Foodi after 25 minutes and dish out to serve.

Nutritional Value:
- Calories 197
- Total Fat 13.8 g
- Saturated Fat 5.8 g
- Cholesterol 37 mg
- Total Carbs 4.7 g
- Sugar 1.9 g
- Fiber 0.6 g
- Sodium 662 mg
- Potassium 184 mg
- Protein 14.3 g

Onion Tofu Scramble

Preparation Time: 8 minutes
Cooking Time: 12 minutes
Servings: 4
Ingredients:
- 4 tablespoons butter
- 2 blocks tofu, pressed and cubed into 1 inch pieces
- Salt and black pepper, to taste
- 1 cup cheddar cheese, grated
- 2 medium onions, sliced

Method:
1. Mix together tofu, salt and black pepper in a bowl.
2. Press "Sauté" on Ninja Foodi and add butter and onions.
3. Sauté for about 3 minutes and add seasoned tofu.
4. Cook for about 2 minutes and add cheddar cheese.
5. Lock the lid and set the Ninja Foodi on "Air Crisp" for about 3 minutes at 340 degrees F.
6. Dish out in a serving plate and serve hot.

Nutritional Value:
- Calories 184
- Total Fat 12.7 g
- Saturated Fat 7.3 g
- Cholesterol 35 mg
- Total Carbs 6.3 g
- Sugar 2.7 g
- Fiber 1.6 g
- Sodium 222 mg
- Potassium 174 mg
- Protein 12.2 g

Pepperoni Omelet

Preparation Time: 5 minutes
Cooking Time: 30 minutes
Servings: 4
Ingredients:
- 4 tablespoons heavy cream
- 15 pepperoni slices
- 2 tablespoons butter
- Salt and black pepper, to taste
- 6 eggs

Method:
1. Whisk together the eggs, heavy cream, pepperoni slices, salt and black pepper in a bowl.
2. Press "Sauté" on Ninja Foodi and add butter and egg mixture.
3. Sauté for about 3 minutes and flip the side of the omelette.
4. Lock the lid and set the Ninja Foodi on "Air Crisp" for about 2 minutes at 350 degrees F.
5. Dish out in a serving plate and serve with low carb bread.

Nutritional Value:
- Calories 141
- Total Fat 11.3 g
- Saturated Fat 3.8 g
- Cholesterol 181 mg
- Total Carbs 0.6 g
- Sugar 0.5 g
- Fiber 0 g
- Sodium 334 mg
- Potassium 103 mg
- Protein 8.9 g

Ham Spinach Ballet

Preparation Time: 5 minutes
Cooking Time: 30 minutes
Servings: 8
Ingredients:
- 3 pounds fresh baby spinach
- ½ cup cream
- 28-ounce ham, sliced
- 4 tablespoons butter, melted
- Salt and freshly ground black pepper, to taste

Method:
1. Press "Sauté" on Ninja Foodi and add butter and spinach.
2. Sauté for about 3 minutes and top with cream, ham slices, salt and black pepper.
3. Lock the lid and set the Ninja Foodi to "Bake/Roast" for about 8 minutes at 360 degrees F.
4. Remove from the Ninja Foodi after 8 minutes and dish out to serve.

Nutritional Value:
- Calories 188
- Total Fat 12.5 g
- Saturated Fat 4.4 g
- Cholesterol 53 mg
- Total Carbs 4.9 g
- Sugar 0.3 g
- Fiber 2 g
- Sodium 1098 mg
- Potassium 484 mg
- Protein 14.6 g

Sausage Solo

Preparation Time: 5 minutes
Cooking Time: 30 minutes
Servings: 4
Ingredients:
- 4 eggs
- 4 cooked sausages, sliced
- 2 tablespoons butter
- ½ cup mozzarella cheese, grated
- ½ cup cream

Method:
1. Mix together eggs and cream in a bowl and beat well.
2. Put the egg mixture in the pot of Ninja Foodi and top evenly with cheese and sausage slices.
3. Press "Bake/Roast" and set the timer to 20 minutes at 345 degrees F.
4. Dish out after 20 minutes and serve immediately.

Nutritional Value:
- Calories 180
- Total Fat 12.7 g
- Saturated Fat 4.7 g
- Cholesterol 264 mg
- Total Carbs 3.9 g
- Sugar 1.3 g
- Fiber 0.1 g
- Sodium 251 mg
- Potassium 142 mg
- Protein 12.4 g

Bacon Bok Choy Samba

Preparation Time: 5 minutes
Cooking Time: 14 minutes
Servings: 6
Ingredients:
- 4 bacon slices
- 2 tablespoons olive oil
- 8 tablespoons cream
- 8 bok choy, sliced
- 1 cup Parmesan cheese, grated
- Salt and black pepper, to taste

Method:
1. Season bok choy with salt and black pepper.
2. Press "Sauté" on Ninja Foodi and add olive oil and bacon slices.
3. Sauté for about 5 minutes and stir in cream and seasoned bok choy.
4. Sauté for about 6 minutes and top with Parmesan cheese.
5. Lock the lid and set the Ninja Foodi on "Air Crisp" for about 3 minutes at 350 degrees F.
6. Dish out in a serving plate and serve hot.

Nutritional Value:
- Calories 112
- Total Fat 4.9 g
- Saturated Fat 1.9 g
- Cholesterol 10 mg
- Total Carbs 1.9 g
- Sugar 0.8 g
- Fiber 0.4 g
- Sodium 355 mg
- Potassium 101 mg
- Protein 3 g

Chapter 6: Snacks and Appetizers Recipes
Eggs Stuffed with Avocado & Watercress

Preparation Time: 10 minutes
Cooking Time: 5 minutes
Servings: 6
Ingredients:
- ½ tablespoon fresh lemon juice
- 1 medium ripe avocado, peeled, pitted and chopped
- 6 organic eggs, boiled, peeled and cut in half lengthwise
- Salt, to taste
- ½ cup fresh watercress, trimmed

Method:
1. Place a steamer basket at the bottom of the Ninja Foodi and pour water.
2. Put the watercress on the basket and lock the lid.
3. Set the Ninja Foodi to "Pressure" for about 3 minutes.
4. Release the pressure quickly and drain the watercress completely.
5. Remove the egg yolks and transfer into a bowl.
6. Add watercress, avocado, lemon juice and salt and mash with a fork completely.
7. Place the egg whites in a serving dish and fill the egg whites with watercress mixture.

Nutritional Value:
- Calories 132
- Total Fat 10.9 g
- Saturated Fat 2.7 g
- Cholesterol 164 mg
- Total Carbs 3.3 g
- Sugar 0.5 g
- Fiber 2.3 g
- Sodium 65 mg
- Potassium 226 mg
- Protein 6.3 g

Cheese Casserole

Preparation Time: 15 minutes
Cooking Time: 22 minutes
Servings: 6
Ingredients:
- 16-ounce marinara sauce
- 10-ounce parmesan, shredded
- 2 tablespoons olive oil
- 16-ounce mozzarella cheese, shredded
- 2 pounds sausages, scrambled

Method:
1. Grease the pot of Ninja Foodi with olive oil and arrange half of the scrambled sausages.
2. Layer with half of the marinara, followed by half of the mozzarella and Parmesan cheese.
3. Top with the remaining half of the scrambled sausages, marinara, mozzarella and Parmesan cheese.
4. Press "Bake/Roast" and set the timer to 20 minutes at 360 degrees F.
5. Remove from the Ninja Foodi after 20 minutes and dish out to serve.

Nutritional Value:
- Calories 521
- Total Fat 38.8 g
- Saturated Fat 12.8 g
- Cholesterol 136 mg
- Total Carbs 6 g
- Sugar 5.4 g
- Fiber 0 g
- Sodium 201 mg
- Potassium 506 mg
- Protein 35.4 g

Avocado Chips

Preparation Time: 10 minutes
Cooking Time: 10 minutes
Servings: 4
Ingredients:
- 4 tablespoons butter
- 4 raw avocados, peeled and sliced in chips form
- Salt and black pepper, to taste

Method:
1. Season the avocado slices with salt and black pepper.
2. Grease the pot of Ninja Foodi with butter and add avocado slices.
3. Press "Air Crisp" and set the timer to 10 minutes at 350 degrees F.
4. Remove from the Ninja Foodi and dish out to serve.

Nutritional Value:
- Calories 391
- Total Fat 38.2 g
- Saturated Fat 11 g
- Cholesterol 31 mg
- Total Carbs 15 g
- Sugar 0.5 g
- Fiber 11.8 g
- Sodium 96 mg
- Potassium 881 mg
- Protein 3.5 g

Scallion Cake

Preparation Time: 10 minutes
Cooking Time: 20 minutes
Servings: 4
Ingredients:
- ½ cup Parmesan cheese, finely grated
- ½ cup low-fat cottage cheese
- ¼ cup flax seeds meal
- ½ teaspoon baking powder
- 1/3 cup scallion, thinly sliced
- ¼ cup nutritional yeast flakes
- ½ cup raw hemp seeds
- Salt, to taste
- ½ cup almond meal
- 6 organic eggs, beaten

Method:
1. Combine eggs and cottage cheese in a bowl and keep aside.
2. Mix together baking powder, hemp seeds, flax seeds meal, almond meal and salt in another bowl.
3. Combine the two mixtures and gently fold in scallion.
4. Transfer the mixture evenly into ramekins and place in the pot of Ninja Foodi.
5. Press "Bake/Roast" and set the timer to 20 minutes at 345 degrees F.
6. Remove from the Ninja Foodi and dish out to serve.

Nutritional Value:
- Calories 306
- Total Fat 19.7 g
- Saturated Fat 4.7 g
- Cholesterol 0 mg
- Total Carbs 10.7 g
- Sugar 1.3 g
- Fiber 4.2 g
- Sodium 398 mg
- Potassium 131 mg

- Protein 23.5 g

Mixed Nuts

Preparation Time: 5 minutes
Cooking Time: 15 minutes
Servings: 5
Ingredients:
- 1 tablespoon butter, melted
- ½ cup raw cashew nuts
- 1 cup raw almonds
- 1 cup raw peanuts
- Salt, to taste

Method:
1. Place the nuts in the pot of Ninja Foodi and lock the lid.
2. Press "Air Crisp" and set the timer to 10 minutes at 350 degrees F.
3. Remove the nuts into a bowl and add melted butter and salt.
4. Toss to coat well and return the nuts mixture into the Ninja Foodi.
5. Press "Bake/Roast" and bake for about 5 minutes.
6. Dish out to serve.

Nutritional Value:
- Calories 189
- Total Fat 16.5 g
- Saturated Fat 2.2 g
- Cholesterol 0 mg
- Total Carbs 6.6 g
- Sugar 1.3 g
- Fiber 2.6 g
- Sodium 19 mg
- Potassium 211 mg
- Protein 6.8 g

Asparagus Bites

Preparation Time: 15 minutes
Cooking Time: 10 minutes
Servings: 3
Ingredients:
- 1 cup asparagus
- ½ cup desiccated coconut
- ½ cup feta cheese

Method:
1. Place the coconut in a shallow dish and coat asparagus with coconut evenly.
2. Place coated asparagus in the pot of Ninja Foodi and top with feta cheese.
3. Press "Air Crisp" and set the timer to 10 minutes at 360 degrees F.
4. Remove from the Ninja Foodi and dish out to serve.

Nutritional Value:
- Calories 135
- Total Fat 10.3 g
- Saturated Fat 7.7 g
- Cholesterol 33 mg
- Total Carbs 5 g
- Sugar 3.1 g
- Fiber 2 g
- Sodium 421 mg
- Potassium 178 mg
- Protein 7 g

Broccoli Pops

Preparation Time: 1 hour
Cooking Time: 12 minutes
Servings: 6
Ingredients:
- 1/3 cup Parmesan cheese, grated
- 2 cups cheddar cheese, grated
- Salt and black pepper, to taste
- 3 eggs, beaten
- 3 cups broccoli florets
- 1 tablespoon olive oil

Method:
1. Put broccoli in a food processor and pulse until crumbed finely.
2. Transfer broccoli in a large bowl with the remaining ingredients and mix until well combined.
3. Make small equal-sized balls from mixture and refrigerate for at least 30 minutes.
4. Place balls in the pot of Ninja Foodi and lock the lid.
5. Press "Air Crisp" and set the timer to 12 minutes at 350 degrees F.
6. Remove from the Ninja Foodi and dish out to serve.

Nutritional Value:
- Calories 162
- Total Fat 12.4 g
- Saturated Fat 7.6 g
- Cholesterol 69 mg
- Total Carbs 1.9 g
- Sugar 0.5 g
- Fiber 0.5 g
- Sodium 263 mg
- Potassium 100 mg
- Protein 11.2 g

Zucchini Cream Cheese Fries

Preparation Time: 10 minutes
Cooking Time: 10 minutes
Servings: 4
Ingredients:
- pound zucchini, sliced into 2 ½-inch sticks
- Salt, to taste
- 1 cup cream cheese
- 2 tablespoons olive oil

Method:
1. Put zucchini in a colander and add salt and cream cheese.
2. Put oil and zucchini in the pot of Ninja Foodi and lock the lid.
3. Press "Air Crisp" and set the timer to 10 minutes at 365 degrees F.
4. Dish out from the Ninja Foodi and serve.

Nutritional Value:
- Calories 374
- Total Fat 36.6 g
- Saturated Fat 18.4 g
- Cholesterol 85 mg
- Total Carbs 7.1 g
- Sugar 2.8 g
- Fiber 1.7 g
- Sodium 294 mg
- Potassium 488 mg
- Protein 7.7 g

Chapter 7: Vegetarian Recipes
Mediterranean Spinach with Cheese

Preparation Time: 5 minutes
Cooking Time: 15 minutes
Servings: 6
Ingredients:
- 4 tablespoons butter
- 2 pounds spinach, chopped and boiled
- Salt and black pepper, to taste
- 2/3 cup Kalamata olives, halved and pitted
- 1½ cups feta cheese, grated
- 4 teaspoons fresh lemon zest, grated

Method:
1- Mix together spinach, butter, salt and black pepper in a bowl.
2- Place the basket in the Ninja Foodi and add seasoned spinach.
3- Press "Air Crisp" and set the timer to 15 minutes at 340 degrees F.
4- Dish out from the Ninja Foodi and stir in the olives, lemon zest and feta cheese to serve.

Nutritional Value:
- Calories 247
- Total Fat 18.7 g
- Saturated Fat 3.3 g
- Cholesterol 5 mg
- Total Carbs 7.2 g
- Sugar 2.3 g
- Fiber 3.9 g
- Sodium 335 mg
- Potassium 726 mg
- Protein 9.9 g

Cheesy Veggies

Preparation Time: 5 minutes
Cooking Time: 30 minutes
Servings: 6
Ingredients:
- 2 onions, sliced thinly
- 2 tomatoes, sliced thinly
- 2 zucchinis, sliced
- 2 teaspoons olive oil
- 2 cups cheddar cheese, grated
- 2 teaspoons mixed dried herbs
- Salt and freshly ground black pepper, to taste

Method:
1. Arrange all the vegetables in the pot of Ninja Foodi and top with olive oil, herbs, cheddar cheese, salt and black pepper.
2. Press "Air Crisp" and set the timer to 30 minutes at 350 degrees F.
3. Dish out from the Ninja Foodi and dish out to serve.

Nutritional Value:
- Calories 305
- Total Fat 22.3 g
- Saturated Fat 13.2 g
- Cholesterol 64 mg
- Total Carbs 8.3 g
- Sugar 4.2 g
- Fiber 2.9 g
- Sodium 370 mg
- Potassium 282 mg
- Protein 15.2 g

Stunning Broccoli Florets

Preparation Time: 10 minutes
Cooking Time: 6 minutes
Servings: 6
Ingredients:
- 4 tablespoons butter, melted
- Salt and black pepper, to taste
- 2 pounds broccoli florets
- 1 cup whipping cream

Method:
1. Arrange the basket in the bottom of Ninja Foodi and add water.
2. Place the broccoli florets on top of the basket and lock the lid.
3. Press "Pressure" and cook for about 5 minutes.
4. Release the pressure quickly and replace the pot with the basket.
5. Transfer the broccoli florets in the pot and top with salt, black pepper and butter.
6. Press "Air Crisp" and cook for about 3 minutes at 360 degrees F.
7. Dish out to serve immediately.

Nutritional Value:
- Calories 178
- Total Fat 14.4 g
- Saturated Fat 8.7 g
- Cholesterol 43 mg
- Total Carbs 9.6 g
- Sugar 2.6 g
- Fiber 3.9 g
- Sodium 111 mg
- Potassium 453 mg
- Protein 4.7 g

Cauliflower Mash

Preparation Time: 10 minutes
Cooking Time: 5 minutes
Servings: 6
Ingredients:
- 1 tablespoon butter, softened
- ½ cup feta cheese
- Salt and black pepper, to taste
- 1 large head cauliflower, chop into large pieces
- 1 garlic clove, minced
- 2 teaspoons fresh chives, minced

Method:
1. Arrange the basket in the bottom of Ninja Foodi and add water.
2. Place the cauliflower pieces on top of the basket and lock the lid.
3. Press "Pressure" and cook for about 5 minutes.
4. Release the pressure quickly and dish out in a bowl.
5. Transfer the cauliflower in an immersion hand blender along with rest of the ingredients.
6. Blend until desired texture is achieved and dish out to serve.

Nutritional Value:
- Calories 124
- Total Fat 9.3 g
- Saturated Fat 6.2 g
- Cholesterol 32 mg
- Total Carbs 6.1 g
- Sugar 3.2 g
- Fiber 2.3 g
- Sodium 333 mg
- Potassium 281 mg
- Protein 5.4 g

Nutty Brussels Sprouts

Preparation Time: 10 minutes
Cooking Time: 6 minutes
Servings: 8
Ingredients:
- 2 pounds Brussels sprouts, trimmed and halved
- 1 cup almonds, chopped
- 1 tablespoon unsalted butter, melted

Method:
1. Arrange the basket in the bottom of Ninja Foodi and add water.
2. Place the Brussels sprout on top of the basket and lock the lid.
3. Press "Pressure" and cook for about 3 minutes.
4. Release the pressure quickly and replace the pot with the basket.
5. Transfer the Brussels sprout in the pot and top with almonds and butter.
6. Press "Air Crisp" and cook for about 3 minutes at 350 degrees F.
7. Dish out to serve.

Nutritional Value:
- Calories 130
- Total Fat 7.8 g
- Saturated Fat 1.5 g
- Cholesterol 39 mg
- Total Carbs 8.9 g
- Sugar 3 g
- Fiber 5.7 g
- Sodium 39 mg
- Potassium 57 mg
- Protein 6.4 g

Luncheon Green Beans

Preparation Time: 10 minutes
Cooking Time: 5 minutes
Servings: 4
Ingredients:
- pound fresh green beans
- 2 tablespoons butter
- 1 garlic clove, minced
- Salt and freshly ground black pepper, to taste
- 1½ cups water

Method:
1. Put all the ingredients in the pot of Ninja Foodi and lock the lid.
2. Press "Pressure" and cook for about 5 minutes.
3. Release the pressure quickly and dish out to serve hot.

Nutritional Value:
- Calories 87
- Total Fat 5.9 g
- Saturated Fat 3.7 g
- Cholesterol 91 mg
- Total Carbs 8.4 g
- Sugar 1.6 g
- Fiber 3.9 g
- Sodium 96 mg
- Potassium 110 mg
- Protein 2.2 g

Vegetable Dinner Casserole

Preparation Time: 10 minutes
Cooking Time: 9 minutes
Servings: 8
Ingredients:
- ½ cup almond flour
- Salt and black pepper, to taste
- 1 medium zucchini, chopped
- 1½ cups mozzarella cheese, shredded
- ½ cup unsweetened almond milk
- 8 large organic eggs
- 1 cup tomato, chopped
- 1 medium green bell pepper, seeded and chopped

Method:
1. Arrange the basket in the bottom of Ninja Foodi and add water.
2. Mix together milk, flour, eggs, salt and black pepper in a bowl and beat until well combined.
3. Add vegetables and cheese and stir to combine.
4. Add the mixture to the baking dish and lock the lid.
5. Press "Pressure" and cook for about 30 minutes.
6. Release the pressure naturally and replace the pot with the basket.
7. Dish out and serve immediately.

Nutritional Value:
- Calories 102
- Total Fat 9.6 g
- Saturated Fat 2.4 g
- Cholesterol 61 mg
- Total Carbs 5.1 g
- Sugar 2.2 g
- Fiber 1.6 g
- Sodium 139 mg
- Potassium 307 mg
- Protein 10 g

Cheesy Cauliflower

Preparation Time: 5 minutes
Cooking Time: 30 minutes
Servings: 5
Ingredients:
- 1 tablespoon prepared mustard
- 1 head cauliflower
- 1 teaspoon avocado mayonnaise
- ½ cup Parmesan cheese, grated
- ¼ cup butter, cut into small pieces

Method:
1. Press "Sauté" on Ninja Foodi and add butter and cauliflower.
2. Sauté for about 3 minutes and add rest of the ingredients.
3. Lock the lid and set the Ninja Foodi to "Pressure" for about 30 minutes.
4. Release the pressure naturally and dish out to serve hot.

Nutritional Value:
- Calories 155
- Total Fat 13.3 g
- Saturated Fat 8.3 g
- Cholesterol 37 mg
- Total Carbs 3.8 g
- Sugar 1.4 g
- Fiber 1.4 g
- Sodium 280 mg
- Potassium 173 mg
- Protein 6.7 g

Chapter 8: Fish and Seafood Recipes
Salmon Stew

Preparation Time: 5 minutes
Cooking Time: 11 minutes
Servings: 3
Ingredients:
- 1 cup homemade fish broth
- Salt and black pepper, to taste
- 1 medium onion, chopped
- pound salmon fillet, cubed
- 1 tablespoon butter

Method:
1. Season the salmon fillets with salt and black pepper.
2. Press "Sauté" on Ninja Foodi and add butter and onions.
3. Sauté for about 3 minutes and add salmon and fish broth.
4. Lock the lid and set the Ninja Foodi to "Pressure" for about 8 minutes.
5. Release the pressure naturally and dish out to serve hot.

Nutritional Value:
- Calories 272
- Total Fat 14.2 g
- Saturated Fat 4.1 g
- Cholesterol 82 mg
- Total Carbs 4.4 g
- Sugar 1.9 g
- Fiber 1.1 g
- Sodium 275 mg
- Potassium 635 mg
- Protein 32.1 g

Paprika Shrimp

Preparation Time: 5 minutes
Cooking Time: 15 minutes
Servings: 3
Ingredients:
- 1 teaspoon smoked paprika
- 3 tablespoons butter
- pound tiger shrimps
- Salt, to taste

Method:
1. Combine all the ingredients in a large bowl and marinate the shrimps in it.
2. Grease the pot of Ninja Foodi with butter and transfer the seasoned shrimps in it.
3. Press "Bake/Roast" and set the timer to 15 minutes at 355 degrees F.
4. Dish out shrimps from the Ninja Foodi and serve.

Nutritional Value:
- Calories 173
- Total Fat 8.3 g
- Saturated Fat 1.3 g
- Cholesterol 221 mg
- Total Carbs 0.1 g
- Sugar 0 g
- Fiber 0.1 g
- Sodium 332 mg
- Potassium 212 mg
- Protein 23.8 g

Ketogenic Butter Fish

Preparation Time: 10 minutes
Cooking Time: 30 minutes
Servings: 3
Ingredients:
- pound salmon fillets
- 2 tablespoons ginger-garlic paste
- 3 green chilies, chopped
- Salt and black pepper, to taste
- ¾ cup butter

Method:
1. Season the salmon fillets with ginger-garlic paste, salt and black pepper.
2. Place the salmon fillets in the pot of Ninja Foodi and top with green chilies and butter.
3. Press "Bake/Roast" and set the timer to 30 minutes at 360 degrees F.
4. Bake for about 30 minutes and dish out the fillets in a serving platter.

Nutritional Value:
- Calories 507
- Total Fat 45.9 g
- Saturated Fat 22.9 g
- Cholesterol 142 mg
- Total Carbs 2.4 g
- Sugar 0.2 g
- Fiber 0.1 g
- Sodium 296 mg
- Potassium 453 mg
- Protein 22.8 g

Shrimp Magic

Preparation Time: 10 minutes
Cooking Time: 15 minutes
Servings: 3
Ingredients:
- 2 tablespoons butter
- ½ teaspoon smoked paprika
- 1-pound shrimps, peeled and deveined
- Lemongrass stalks
- 1 red chili pepper, seeded and chopped

Method:
1. Mix together all the ingredients in a bowl except lemongrass and marinate for about 1 hour.
2. Press "Bake/Roast" and set the timer to 15 minutes at 345 degrees F.
3. Bake for about 15 minutes and dish out the fillets.

Nutritional Value:
- Calories 251
- Total Fat 10.3 g
- Saturated Fat 5.7 g
- Cholesterol 339 mg
- Total Carbs 3 g
- Sugar 0.1 g
- Fiber 0.2 g
- Sodium 424 mg
- Potassium 281 mg
- Protein 34.6 g

Sweet and Sour Fish

Preparation Time: 10 minutes
Cooking Time: 6 minutes
Servings: 3
Ingredients:
- 2 drops liquid stevia
- ¼ cup butter
- 1-pound fish chunks
- 1 tablespoon vinegar
- Salt and black pepper, to taste

Method:
1. Press "Sauté" on Ninja Foodi and add butter and fish chunks.
2. Sauté for about 3 minutes and add stevia, salt and black pepper.
3. Press "Air Crisp" and cook for about 3 minutes at 360 degrees F.
4. Dish out in a serving bowl and serve immediately.

Nutritional Value:
- Calories 274
- Total Fat 15.4 g
- Saturated Fat 9.7 g
- Cholesterol 54 mg
- Total Carbs 2.8 g
- Sugar 0 g
- Fiber 0 g
- Sodium 604 mg
- Potassium 8 mg
- Protein 33.2 g

Buttered Scallops

Preparation Time: 10 minutes
Cooking Time: 15 minutes
Servings: 6
Ingredients:
- 4 garlic cloves, minced
- 4 tablespoons fresh rosemary, chopped
- 2 pounds sea scallops
- ½ cup butter
- Salt and black pepper, to taste

Method:
1. Press "Sauté" on Ninja Foodi and add butter, rosemary and garlic.
2. Sauté for about 1 minute and add sea scallops, salt and black pepper.
3. Sauté for about 2 minutes and press "Air Crisp" at 350 degrees F.
4. Set the timer for about 3 minutes and dish out to serve.

Nutritional Value:
- Calories 279
- Total Fat 16.8 g
- Saturated Fat 10 g
- Cholesterol 91 mg
- Total Carbs 5.7 g
- Sugar 0 g
- Fiber 1 g
- Sodium 354 mg
- Potassium 520 mg
- Protein 25.8 g

Buffalo Fish

Preparation Time: 10 minutes
Cooking Time: 11 minutes
Servings: 6
Ingredients:
- 6 tablespoons butter
- ¾ cup Franks red hot sauce
- 6 fish fillets
- Salt and black pepper, to taste
- 2 teaspoons garlic powder

Method:
1. Press "Sauté" on Ninja Foodi and add butter and fish fillets.
2. Sauté for about 3 minutes and add salt, black pepper and garlic powder.
3. Press "Bake/Roast" and bake for about 8 minutes at 340 degrees F.
4. Dish out in a serving platter and serve hot.

Nutritional Value:
- Calories 317
- Total Fat 22.7 g
- Saturated Fat 9.9 g
- Cholesterol 61 mg
- Total Carbs 16.4 g
- Sugar 0.2 g
- Fiber 0.6 g
- Sodium 659 mg
- Potassium 307 mg
- Protein 13.6 g

Cod: Battle of Herbs

Preparation Time: 5 minutes
Cooking Time: 8 minutes
Servings: 6
Ingredients:
- 4 garlic cloves, minced
- 2 teaspoons soy sauce
- ¼ cup butter
- 6 eggs
- 2 small onions, chopped finely
- 3 (4-ounce) skinless cod fish fillets, cut into rectangular pieces
- 2 green chilies, chopped finely
- Salt and black pepper, to taste

Method:
1. Combine all the ingredients in a shallow dish except cod and beat well.
2. Dip each fillet in this mixture and set aside.
3. Transfer the fillets in the basket and lock the lid.
4. Press "Air Crisp" and cook for about 8 minutes at 330 degrees F.
5. Dish out and serve hot.

Nutritional Value:
- Calories 409
- Total Fat 25.2 g
- Saturated Fat 12.6 g
- Cholesterol 430 mg
- Total Carbs 7 g
- Sugar 3 g
- Fiber 1.1 g
- Sodium 363 mg
- Potassium 483 mg
- Protein 37.9 g

Chapter9: Poultry Recipes
Creamy Chicken Breasts

Preparation Time: 10 minutes
Cooking Time: 15 minutes
Servings: 4
Ingredients:
- 1 small onion
- 2 tablespoons butter
- pound chicken breasts
- ½ cup sour cream
- Salt, to taste

Method:
1. Season the chicken breasts generously with salt and keep aside.
2. Heat butter in a skillet on medium-low heat and add onions.
3. Sauté for 3 minutes and add chicken breasts.
4. Cover the lid and cook for about 10 minutes.
5. Stir in the sour cream and cook for about 4 minutes.
6. Stir gently and dish out to serve.

Nutritional Value:
- Calories 447
- Total Fat 26.9 g
- Saturated Fat 12.9 g
- Cholesterol 172 mg
- Total Carbs 3.8 g
- Sugar 1.1 g
- Fiber 0.5 g
- Sodium 206 mg
- Potassium 459 mg
- Protein 45.3 g

Chicken Ropa Vieja

Preparation Time: 5 minutes
Cooking Time: 4 hours 8 minutes
Servings: 4
Ingredients:
- 3 tablespoons butter
- ½ yellow onion, sliced into long strips
- 1 tablespoon tomato paste
- 1/8 teaspoon red pepper flakes
- 1½ pounds chicken pieces, boneless and skinless
- ½ tablespoon oregano
- ½ red bell pepper, sliced into long strips
- 3 garlic cloves, minced
- ½ teaspoon cumin powder
- ½ green bell pepper, sliced into long strips
- Salt and black pepper, to taste
- ½ cup tomatoes, diced

Method:
1. Season the chicken pieces with cumin powder, oregano, salt, black pepper and red pepper flakes.
2. Press "Sauté" on Ninja Foodi and add butter and seasoned chicken.
3. Sauté for about 2 minutes and add onions, red bell pepper and green bell pepper.
4. Sauté for about 1 minute and add diced tomatoes, garlic and tomato paste.
5. Lock the lid and press "Slow Cooker" on high for about 4 hours.
6. Remove the lid after 4 hours and break the chicken pieces stirring thoroughly.
7. Press "Air Crisp" and cook for about 5 minutes at 360 degrees F.
8. Dish out to serve hot.

Nutritional Value:
- Calories 285
- Total Fat 11.2 g
- Saturated Fat 5.5 g
- Cholesterol 122 mg
- Total Carbs 6 g

- Sugar 3 g
- Fiber 1.4 g
- Sodium 182 mg
- Potassium 130 mg
- Protein 40.6 g

Ham Stuffed Turkey Rolls

Preparation Time: 10 minutes
Cooking Time: 20 minutes
Servings: 8
Ingredients:
- 4 tablespoons fresh sage leaves
- 8 ham slices
- 8 (6-ounce) turkey cutlets
- Salt and black pepper, to taste
- 2 tablespoons butter, melted

Method:
1. Season the turkey cutlets with salt and black pepper.
2. Roll the turkey cutlets and wrap each one with ham slices tightly.
3. Coat each roll with butter and place the sage leaves evenly over each cutlet.
4. Press "Bake/Roast" on Ninja Foodi and add turkey rolls.
5. Bake for about 10 minutes at 360 degrees F and flip the sides.
6. Bake for another 10 minutes and dish out to serve.

Nutritional Value:
- Calories 467
- Total Fat 24.8 g
- Saturated Fat 10 g
- Cholesterol 218 mg
- Total Carbs 1.7 g
- Sugar 0 g
- Fiber 0.8 g
- Sodium 534 mg
- Potassium 645 mg
- Protein 56 g

Stuffed Whole Chicken

Preparation Time: 10 minutes
Cooking Time: 8 hours
Servings: 6
Ingredients:
- 1 cup mozzarella cheese
- 4 whole garlic cloves, peeled
- 1 (2-pound) whole chicken, cleaned, pat dried
- Salt and black pepper, to taste
- 2 tablespoons fresh lemon juice

Method:
1. Stuff the chicken cavity with garlic cloves mozzarella cheese.
2. Season the chicken with salt and black pepper.
3. Transfer the chicken in the Ninja Foodi and drizzle lemon juice.
4. Press "Slow Cooker" and cook on Low for about 8 hours.
5. Dish out and serve hot.

Nutritional Value:
- Calories 309
- Total Fat 12.1 g
- Saturated Fat 3.6 g
- Cholesterol 137 mg
- Total Carbs 1.6 g
- Sugar 0.7 g
- Fiber 0.8 g
- Sodium 201 mg
- Potassium 390 mg
- Protein 45.8 g

Creamy Turkey Breast

Preparation Time: 10 minutes
Cooking Time: 2 hours
Servings: 6
Ingredients:
- 1½ cups Italian dressing
- 2 garlic cloves, minced
- 1 (2-pound) bone-in turkey breast
- 2 tablespoons butter
- Salt and black pepper, to taste

Method:
1. Mix together garlic cloves, salt and black pepper and rub the turkey breast with this mixture.
2. Grease the pot of Ninja Foodi with butter and arrange turkey breasts.
3. Top evenly with Italian dressing and press "Bake/Roast".
4. Bake for about 2 hours at 330 degrees F and dish out to serve immediately.

Nutritional Value:
- Calories 369
- Total Fat 23.2 g
- Saturated Fat 5.1 g
- Cholesterol 104 mg
- Total Carbs 6.5 g
- Sugar 4.9 g
- Fiber 0 g
- Sodium 990 mg
- Potassium 33 mg
- Protein 35.4 g

Caprese Hasselback Chicken

Preparation Time: 10 minutes
Cooking Time: 1 hour
Servings: 8
Ingredients:
- 4 tablespoons butter
- Salt and black pepper, to taste
- 2 cups fresh mozzarella cheese, thinly sliced
- 8 large chicken breasts
- 4 large roma tomatoes, thinly sliced

Method:
1. Make a few deep slits in the chicken breasts and season with salt and black pepper.
2. Stuff the mozzarella cheese slices and tomatoes in the chicken slits.
3. Grease the pot of Ninja Foodi with butter and arrange stuffed chicken breasts.
4. Press "Bake/Roast" and bake for about 1 hour at 365 degrees F.
5. Dish out and serve hot.

Nutritional Value:
- Calories 287
- Total Fat 15 g
- Saturated Fat 6.6 g
- Cholesterol 112 mg
- Total Carbs 3.8 g
- Sugar 2.4 g
- Fiber 1.1 g
- Sodium 178 mg
- Potassium 473 mg
- Protein 33.2 g

Mediterranean Turkey Cutlets

Preparation Time: 10 minutes
Cooking Time: 15 minutes
Servings: 4
Ingredients:
- 1 teaspoon Greek seasoning
- 1-pound turkey cutlets
- 2 tablespoons olive oil
- 1 teaspoon turmeric powder
- ½ cup almond flour

Method:
1. Combine Greek seasoning, turmeric powder and almond flour in a bowl.
2. Dredge turkey cutlets in it and set aside for about 30 minutes.
3. Press "Sauté" on Ninja Foodi and add oil and turkey cutlets.
4. Sauté for about 2 minutes and add turkey cutlets.
5. Press "Pressure" and set to "Lo:Md" for about 20 minutes.
6. Dish out in a serving platter.

Nutritional Value:
- Calories 340
- Total Fat 19.4 g
- Saturated Fat 3.4 g
- Cholesterol 86 mg
- Total Carbs 3.7 g
- Sugar 0 g
- Fiber 1.6 g
- Sodium 124 mg
- Potassium 356 mg
- Protein 36.3 g

Keto Garlic Turkey Breasts

Preparation Time: 10 minutes
Cooking Time: 17 minutes
Servings: 4
Ingredients:
- ½ teaspoon garlic powder
- 4 tablespoons butter
- ¼ teaspoon dried oregano
- 1-pound turkey breasts, boneless
- 1 teaspoon black pepper
- ½ teaspoon salt
- ¼ teaspoon dried basil

Method:
1. Season the turkey on both sides with garlic powder, dried oregano, dried basil, salt and black pepper.
2. Press "Sauté" on Ninja Foodi and add butter and turkey breasts.
3. Sauté for about 2 minutes on each side and lock the lid.
4. Press "Bake/Roast" and bake for about 15 minutes at 355 degrees F.
5. Dish out in a platter and serve hot.

Nutritional Value:
- Calories 223
- Total Fat 13.4 g
- Saturated Fat 7.7 g
- Cholesterol 79 mg
- Total Carbs 5.4 g
- Sugar 4.1 g
- Fiber 0.8 g
- Sodium 1524 mg
- Potassium 358 mg
- Protein 19.6 g

Chili Lime Chicken

Preparation Time: 10 minutes
Cooking Time: 23 minutes
Servings: 6
Ingredients:
- ¼ cup cooking wine
- ½ cup organic chicken broth
- 1 onion, diced
- 1 teaspoon sea salt
- ½ teaspoon paprika
- 5 garlic cloves, minced
- 1 tablespoon lime juice
- ¼ cup butter
- 2 pounds chicken thighs
- 1 teaspoon dried parsley
- 3 green chilies, chopped

Directions:
1. Press "Sauté" on Ninja Foodi and add onions and garlic.
2. Sauté for about 3 minutes and add rest of the ingredients.
3. Press "Pressure" and set the timer to 20 minutes on "Md:Hi".
4. Transfer to a platter and serve hot.

Nutritional Value:
- Calories 282
- Total Fat 15.2 g
- Saturated Fat 7.2 g
- Cholesterol 129 mg
- Total Carbs 6.3 g
- Sugar 3.3 g
- Fiber 0.9 g
- Sodium 2117 mg
- Potassium 511 mg
- Protein 27.4 g

Chapter 10: Beef, Pork and Lamb Recipes
Garlic Creamy Beef Steak

Preparation Time: 1 hour
Cooking Time: 30 minutes
Servings: 6
Ingredients:
- ½ cup butter
- 4 garlic cloves, minced
- 2 pounds beef top sirloin steaks
- Salt and black pepper, to taste
- 1½ cup cream

Method:
1. Rub the beef sirloin steaks with garlic, salt and black pepper.
2. Marinate the beef with butter and cream and set aside.
3. Place grill in the Ninja Foodi and transfer the steaks on it.
4. Press "Broil" and set the timer for about 30 minutes at 365 degrees F, flipping once in the middle way.
5. Dish out and serve hot.

Nutritional Value:
- Calories 353
- Total Fat 24.1 g
- Saturated Fat 14.5 g
- Cholesterol 113 mg
- Total Carbs 3.9 g
- Sugar 1.2 g
- Fiber 0 g
- Sodium 298 mg
- Potassium 35 mg
- Protein 31.8 g

Ketogenic Beef Sirloin Steak

Preparation Time: 5 minutes
Cooking Time: 17 minutes
Servings: 3
Ingredients:
- 3 tablespoons butter
- ½ teaspoon garlic powder
- pound beef top sirloin steaks
- Salt and black pepper, to taste
- 1 garlic clove, minced

Method:
1. Press "Sauté" on Ninja Foodi and add butter and beef sirloin steaks.
2. Sauté for about 2 minutes on each side and add garlic powder, garlic clove, salt and black pepper.
3. Press "Pressure" and set the timer to 15 minutes on "Md:Hi".
4. Transfer the steaks in a serving platter and serve hot.

Nutritional Value:
- Calories 246
- Total Fat 13.1 g
- Saturated Fat 7.6 g
- Cholesterol 81 mg
- Total Carbs 2 g
- Sugar 0.1 g
- Fiber 0.1 g
- Sodium 224 mg
- Potassium 11 mg
- Protein 31.3 g

Bacon Swiss Pork Chops

Preparation Time: 5 minutes
Cooking Time: 18 minutes
Servings: 4
Ingredients:
- ½ cup Swiss cheese, shredded
- 4 pork chops, bone-in
- 6 bacon strips, cut in half
- Salt and black pepper, to taste
- 1 tablespoon butter

Method:
1. Season the pork chops generously with salt and black pepper.
2. Press "Sauté" on Ninja Foodi and add butter and pork chops.
3. Sauté for about 3 minutes on each side and add bacon strips and Swiss cheese.
4. Press "Pressure" and set the timer to 15 minutes on Medium Low.
5. Transfer the steaks in a serving platter and serve hot.

Nutritional Value:
- Calories 483
- Total Fat 40 g
- Saturated Fat 16.2 g
- Cholesterol 89 mg
- Total Carbs 0.7 g
- Sugar 0.2 g
- Fiber 0 g
- Sodium 552 mg
- Potassium 286 mg
- Protein 27.7 g

Crock Pot Beef Fajitas

Preparation Time: 5 minutes
Cooking Time: 7 hours 3 minutes
Servings: 8
Ingredients:
- 2 tablespoons butter
- 2 bell peppers, sliced
- 2 pounds beef, sliced
- 2 tablespoons fajita seasoning
- 2 onions, sliced

Method:
1. Press "Sauté" on Ninja Foodi and add butter, onions, fajita seasoning, bell pepper and beef.
2. Sauté for about 3 minutes and press "Slow Cooker".
3. Cook on Low for about 7 hours and dish out to serve hot.

Nutritional Value:
- Calories 353
- Total Fat 13.4 g
- Saturated Fat 6 g
- Cholesterol 145 mg
- Total Carbs 8.5 g
- Sugar 3.6 g
- Fiber 1.3 g
- Sodium 304 mg
- Potassium 738 mg
- Protein 46.7 g

Jamaican Jerk Pork Roast

Preparation Time: 10 minutes
Cooking Time: 23 minutes
Servings: 3
Ingredients:
- 1 tablespoon butter
- 1/8 cup beef broth
- 1-pound pork shoulder
- 1/8 cup Jamaican jerk spice blend

Method:
1. Season the pork with Jamaican jerk spice blend.
2. Press "Sauté" on Ninja Foodi and add butter and seasoned pork.
3. Sauté for about 3 minutes and add beef broth.
4. Press "Pressure" and cook for about 20 minutes on Low.
5. Release the pressure naturally and dish out in a platter.

Nutritional Value:
- Calories 477
- Total Fat 36.2 g
- Saturated Fat 14.3 g
- Cholesterol 146 mg
- Total Carbs 0 g
- Sugar 0 g
- Fiber 0 g
- Sodium 162 mg
- Potassium 507 mg
- Protein 35.4 g

Crispy Pork Carnitas

Preparation Time: 10 minutes
Cooking Time: 26 minutes
Servings: 6
Ingredients:
- 2 tablespoons butter
- 2 oranges, juiced
- 2 pounds pork shoulder, bone-in
- Salt and black pepper, to taste
- 1 teaspoon garlic powder

Directions:
1. Season the pork with salt and black pepper.
2. Press "Sauté" on Ninja Foodi and add butter and garlic powder.
3. Sauté for about 1 minute and add seasoned pork.
4. Sauté for 3 minutes and pour orange juice.
5. Press "Pressure" and cook for about 15 minutes on High.
6. Release the pressure naturally and press "Broil".
7. Broil for about 8 minutes at 375 degrees F and dish out to serve.

Nutritional Value:
- Calories 506
- Total Fat 36.3 g
- Saturated Fat 14.3 g
- Cholesterol 146 mg
- Total carbs 7.6 g
- Sugar 5.8 g
- Fiber 1.5 g
- Sodium 130 mg
- Potassium 615 mg
- Protein 35.9 g

Mexican Taco Casserole

Preparation Time: 10 minutes
Cooking Time: 25 minutes
Servings: 6
Ingredients:
- 1 cup cheddar cheese, shredded
- 1 cup cottage cheese
- 2 pounds ground beef
- 1 cup salsa
- 2 tablespoons taco seasoning

Directions:
1. Mix together the taco seasoning and ground beef in a bowl.
2. Stir in salsa, cottage cheese and cheddar cheese.
3. Place ground beef mixture in the pot of Ninja Foodi and lock the lid.
4. Press "Bake/Roast" and set the timer to about 25 minutes at 370 degrees F.
5. Bake for about 25 minutes and dish out to serve immediately.

Nutritional Value:
- Calories 409
- Total Fat 16.5 g
- Saturated Fat 8 g
- Cholesterol 158 mg
- Total Carbs 5.7 g
- Sugar 1.9 g
- Fiber 0.6 g
- Sodium 769 mg
- Potassium 792 mg
- Protein 56.4 g

Mustard Pork Chops

Preparation Time: 10 minutes
Cooking Time: 30 minutes
Servings: 4
Ingredients:
- 2 tablespoons butter
- 2 tablespoons Dijon mustard
- 4 pork chops
- Salt and black pepper, to taste
- 1 tablespoon fresh rosemary, coarsely chopped

Method:
1. Marinate the pork chops with Dijon mustard, fresh rosemary, salt and black pepper for about 2 hours.
2. Put the butter and marinated pork chops in the pot of Ninja Foodi and cover the lid.
3. Press "Pressure" and cook for about 30 minutes on Lo:Md.
4. Release the pressure naturally and dish out in a platter.

Nutritional Value:
- Calories 315
- Total Fat 26.1 g
- Saturated Fat 11.2 g
- Cholesterol 84 mg
- Total Carbs 1 g
- Sugar 0.1 g
- Fiber 0.6 g
- Sodium 186 mg
- Potassium 296 mg
- Protein 18.4 g

Zesty Lamb Chops

Preparation Time: 10 minutes
Cooking Time: 42 minutes
Servings: 4
Ingredients:
- 4 tablespoons butter
- 3 tablespoons lemon juice
- 4 lamb chops, bone-in
- 2 tablespoons almond flour
- 1 cup picante sauce

Method:
1. Coat the chops with almond flour and keep aside.
2. Press "Sauté" on Ninja Foodi and add butter and chops.
3. Sauté for about 2 minutes and add picante sauce and lemon juice.
4. Press "Pressure" and set the timer for 40 minutes at "Hi".
5. Release the pressure naturally and dish out to serve hot.

Nutritional Value:
- Calories 284
- Total Fat 19.5 g
- Saturated Fat 9.7 g
- Cholesterol 107 mg
- Total Carbs 1 g
- Sugar 0.3 g
- Fiber 0.4 g
- Sodium 150 mg
- Potassium 302 mg
- Protein 24.8 g

Lamb Roast

Preparation Time: 10 minutes
Cooking Time: 1 hour
Servings: 6
Ingredients:
- 2 pounds lamb roasted wegmans
- 1 cup onion soup
- 1 cups beef broth
- Salt and black pepper, to taste

Method:
1. Put the lamb roast in the pot of Ninja Foodi and add onion soup, beef broth, salt and black pepper.
2. Lock the lid and set the Ninja Foodi to "Pressure" for about 55 minutes at "Md:Hi".
3. Release the pressure naturally and dish out.

Nutritional Value:
- Calories 349
- Total Fat 18.8 g
- Saturated Fat 0.2 g
- Cholesterol 122 mg
- Total Carbs 2.9 g
- Sugar 1.2 g
- Fiber 0.3 g
- Sodium 480 mg
- Potassium 57 mg
- Protein 39.9 g

Keto Lamb Minced Meat

Preparation Time: 10 minutes
Cooking Time: 23 minutes
Servings: 4
Ingredients:
- 2 tablespoons butter
- ½ teaspoon turmeric powder
- 1-pound ground lamb meat
- 1 cup onions, chopped
- 1 teaspoon salt
- 1 tablespoon garlic, minced
- ½ teaspoon ground coriander
- ½ teaspoon cayenne pepper
- 1 tablespoon ginger, minced
- ½ teaspoon cumin powder

Method:
1. Press "Sauté" on Ninja Foodi and add garlic, ginger and onions.
2. Sauté for about 3 minutes and add ground meat and all the spices.
3. Lock the lid and set the Ninja Foodi to "Pressure" for about 20 minutes at "Md:Hi".
4. Release the pressure naturally and dish out in a large serving bowl.

Nutritional Value:
- Calories 304
- Total Fat 21.1 g
- Saturated Fat 10.7 g
- Cholesterol 96 mg
- Total Carbs 4.8 g
- Sugar 1.3 g
- Fiber 1 g
- Sodium 705 mg
- Potassium 87 mg
- Protein 21.8 g

Greek Lamb Gyros

Preparation Time: 10 minutes
Cooking Time: 25 minutes
Servings: 8
Ingredients:
- 8 garlic cloves
- 1½ teaspoons salt
- 2 teaspoons dried oregano
- 1½ cups water
- 2 pounds lamb meat, ground
- 2 teaspoons rosemary
- ½ teaspoon black pepper
- 1 small onion, chopped
- 2 teaspoons ground marjoram

Method:
1. Put onions, garlic, marjoram, rosemary, salt and black pepper in a food processor and process until combined.
2. Add ground lamb meat and process again.
3. Press meat mixture into the Loaf Pan until tight and compact.
4. Place the meat loaf in the pot of Ninja Foodi and press "Bake/Roast".
5. Bake for about 25 minutes at 375 degrees F and dish out in a platter.

Nutritional Value:
- Calories 242
- Total Fat 15.2 g
- Saturated Fat 7.1 g
- Cholesterol 80 mg
- Total Carbs 2.4 g
- Sugar 0.4 g
- Fiber 0.6 g
- Sodium 521 mg
- Potassium 38 mg
- Protein 21.4 g

Indian Beef

Preparation Time: 15 minutes
Cooking Time: 20 minutes
Servings: 4
Ingredients:
- ½ yellow onion, chopped
- 1 tablespoon olive oil
- 2 garlic cloves, minced
- 1 jalapeño pepper, chopped
- 1 cup cherry tomatoes, quartered
- 1 teaspoon fresh lemon juice
- pound grass-fed ground beef
- pound fresh collard greens, trimmed and chopped

Spices
- 1 teaspoon ground cumin
- ½ teaspoon ground ginger
- 1 teaspoon ground coriander
- ½ teaspoon ground fennel seeds
- ½ teaspoon ground cinnamon
- Salt and black pepper, to taste
- ½ teaspoon ground turmeric

Directions:
1. Press "Sauté" on Ninja Foodi and add garlic and onions.
2. Sauté for about 3 minutes and add jalapeño peppers, beef and spices.
3. Lock the lid and set the Ninja Foodi to "Pressure" for about 15 minutes at "Md:Hi".
4. Release the pressure naturally and add cherry tomatoes and collard greens.
5. Press "Sauté" and sauté for about 3 minutes.
6. Stir in lemon juice, salt and black pepper and dish out in a serving bowl.

Nutritional Value:
- Calories 409
- Total Fat 16.5 g
- Saturated Fat 8 g

- Cholesterol 158 mg
- Total Carbs 5.7 g
- Sugar 1.9 g
- Fiber 0.6 g
- Sodium 769 mg
- Potassium 792 mg
- Protein 56.4 g

Classical Steak Meal

Preparation Time: 20 minutes
Cooking Time: 27 minutes
Servings: 4
Ingredients:
For Steak Sauce:
- 2 tablespoons yellow onion
- 2 tablespoons butter
- 2 garlic cloves, minced
- 1½ cups homemade beef broth
- ¾ cup fresh blueberries
- 1 teaspoon fresh thyme, chopped finely
- 2 tablespoons fresh lemon juice

For Steak:
- 4 (6-ounce) grass-fed flank steaks
- 1 tablespoon butter
- Salt and black pepper, to taste

Directions:
For Sauce:
1. Press "Sauté" on Ninja Foodi and add butter, thyme, garlic and onions.
2. Sauté for about 3 minutes and add broth.
3. Lock the lid and set the Ninja Foodi to "Pressure" for about 10 minutes at Medium Low.
4. Release the pressure naturally and stir in the blueberries, lemon juice, salt and black pepper.
5. Press "Sauté" and sauté for about 2 minutes and transfer in a bowl.

For Steak:
1. Press "Sauté" on Ninja Foodi and add butter, steaks, salt and black pepper.
2. Sauté for about 2 minutes and lock the lid.
3. Set the Ninja Foodi to "Pressure" for about 10 minutes at Medium High.
4. Release the pressure naturally and dish out in a plate.
5. Pour the topping over the steaks and enjoy.

Nutritional Value:

- Calories 409
- Total Fat 16.5 g
- Saturated Fat 8 g
- Cholesterol 158 mg
- Total Carbs 5.7 g
- Sugar 1.9 g
- Fiber 0.6 g
- Sodium 769 mg
- Potassium 792 mg
- Protein 56.4 g

Meat Loaf

Preparation Time: 10 minutes
Cooking Time: 1 hour 10 minutes
Servings: 6
Ingredients:
- ½ cup onion, chopped
- 2 garlic cloves, minced
- ¼ cup sugar-free ketchup
- 1-pound grass-fed lean ground beef
- ½ cup green bell pepper, seeded and chopped
- 1 cup cheddar cheese, grated
- 2 organic eggs, beaten
- 1 teaspoon dried thyme, crushed
- 3 cups fresh spinach, chopped
- 6 cups mozzarella cheese, freshly grated
- Black pepper, to taste

Directions:
1. Combine all the ingredients in a bowl except cheese and spinach.
2. Place a wax paper on a smooth surface and arrange meat over it.
3. Top with spinach and cheese and roll up the paper around the mixture to form a meatloaf.
4. Remove the wax paper and place the meat loaf in the pot of Ninja Foodi.
5. Press "Bake/Roast" and set the timer for about 70 minutes at 380 degrees F.
6. Dish out after 70 minutes and dish out to serve.

Nutritional Value:
- Calories 409
- Total Fat 16.5 g
- Saturated Fat 8 g
- Cholesterol 158 mg
- Total Carbs 5.7 g
- Sugar 1.9 g
- Fiber 0.6 g
- Sodium 769 mg

- Potassium 792 mg
- Protein 56.4 g

Chapter 11: Desserts Recipes
Chocolate Peanut Butter Cups

Preparation Time: 10 minutes
Cooking Time: 30 minutes
Servings: 3
Ingredients:
- 1 cup butter
- ¼ cup heavy cream
- 2 ounces unsweetened chocolate
- ¼ cup peanut butter, separated
- 4 packets stevia

Method:
1. Melt the peanut butter and butter in a bowl and stir in unsweetened chocolate, stevia and heavy cream.
2. Mix thoroughly and pour the mixture in a baking mold.
3. Put the baking mold in the Ninja Foodi and press "Bake/Roast".
4. Set the timer for about 30 minutes at 360 degrees F and dish out to serve.

Nutritional Value:
- Calories 479
- Total Fat 51.5 g
- Saturated Fat 29.7 g
- Cholesterol 106 mg
- Total Carbs 7.7 g
- Sugar 1.4 g
- Fiber 2.7 g
- Sodium 69 mg
- Potassium 193 mg
- Protein 5.2 g

Crème Brûlée

Preparation Time: 10 minutes
Cooking Time: 15 minutes
Servings: 4
Ingredients:
- 1 cup heavy cream
- ½ tablespoon vanilla extract
- 3 egg yolks
- 1 pinch salt
- ¼ cup stevia

Method:
1. Mix together egg yolks, vanilla extract, heavy cream and salt in a bowl and beat until combined.
2. Divide the mixture into 4 greased ramekins evenly and transfer the ramekins in the basket of Ninja Foodi.
3. Press "Bake/Roast" and set the timer for about 15 minutes at 365 degrees F.
4. Remove from the Ninja Foodi and cover the ramekins with a plastic wrap.
5. Refrigerate to chill for about 3 hours and serve chilled.

Nutritional Value:
- Calories 149
- Total Fat 14.5 g
- Saturated Fat 8.1 g
- Cholesterol 56 mg
- Total Carbs 1.6 g
- Sugar 0.3 g
- Fiber 0 g
- Sodium 56 mg
- Potassium 39 mg
- Protein 2.6 g

Flourless Chocolate Brownies

Preparation Time: 10 minutes
Cooking Time: 32 minutes
Servings: 4
Ingredients:
- 3 eggs
- ½ cup butter
- ½ cup sugar-free chocolate chips
- 2 scoops stevia
- 1 teaspoon vanilla extract

Directions:
1. Whisk together eggs, stevia and vanilla extract.
2. Transfer this mixture in the blender and blend until frothy.
3. Put the butter and chocolate in the pot of Ninja Foodi and press "Sauté".
4. Sauté for about 2 minutes until the chocolate is melted.
5. Add the melted chocolate mixture to the egg mixture.
6. Pour the mixture in the baking mold and transfer the baking mold in the Ninja Foodi.
7. Press "Bake/Roast" and set the timer for about 30 minutes at 360 degrees F.
8. Bake for about 30 minutes and dish out.
9. Cut into equal square pieces and serve with whipped cream.

Nutritional Information per Serving:
- Calories 266
- Total Fat 26.9 g
- Saturated Fat 15.8 g
- Cholesterol 184 mg
- Total Carbs 2.5 g
- Sugar 0.4 g
- Fiber 0 g
- Sodium 218 mg
- Potassium 53 mg
- Protein 4.5 g

Cream Crepes

Preparation Time: 10 minutes
Cooking Time: 16 minutes
Servings: 6
Ingredients:
- 1½ teaspoons Splenda
- 3 organic eggs
- 3 tablespoons coconut flour
- ½ cup heavy cream
- 3 tablespoons coconut oil, melted and divided

Method:
1. Mix together 1½ tablespoons of coconut oil, Splenda, eggs and salt in a bowl and beat until well combined.
2. Add the coconut flour slowly and continuously beat.
3. Stir in the heavy cream and beat continuously until well combined.
4. Press "Sauté" on Ninja Foodi and pour about ¼ of the mixture in the pot.
5. Sauté for about 2 minutes on each side and dish out.
6. Repeat with the remaining mixture in batches and serve.

Nutritional Value:
- Calories 145
- Total Fat 13.1 g
- Saturated Fat 9.1 g
- Cholesterol 96 mg
- Total Carbs 4 g
- Sugar 1.2 g
- Fiber 1.5 g
- Sodium 35 mg
- Potassium 37 mg
- Protein 3.5 g

Nut Porridge

Preparation Time: 10 minutes
Cooking Time: 10 minutes
Servings: 4
Ingredients:
- 4 teaspoons coconut oil, melted
- 1 cup pecans, halved
- 2 cups water
- 2 tablespoons stevia
- 1 cup cashew nuts, raw and unsalted

Method:
1. Put the cashew nuts and pecans in the food processor and pulse until chunked.
2. Put the nuts mixture into the pot and stir in water, coconut oil and stevia.
3. Press "Sauté" on Ninja Foodi and cook for about 15 minutes.
4. Dish out and serve immediately.

Nutritional Value:
- Calories 260
- Total Fat 22.9 g
- Saturated Fat 7.3 g
- Cholesterol 0 mg
- Total Carbs 12.7 g
- Sugar 1.8 g
- Fiber 1.4 g
- Sodium 9 mg
- Potassium 209 mg
- Protein 5.6 g

Lemon Mousse

Preparation Time: 10 minutes
Cooking Time: 12 minutes
Servings: 2
Ingredients:
- ounce cream cheese, softened
- ½ cup heavy cream
- 1/8 cup fresh lemon juice
- ½ teaspoon lemon liquid stevia
- 2 pinches salt

Method:
1- Mix together cream cheese, heavy cream, lemon juice, salt and stevia in a bowl.
2- Pour into the ramekins and transfer the ramekins in the pot of Ninja Foodi.
3- Press "Bake/Roast" and bake for about 12 minutes at 350 degrees F.
4- Pour into the serving glasses and refrigerate for at least 3 hours before serving.

Nutritional Value:
- Calories 305
- Total Fat 31 g
- Saturated Fat 19.5 g
- Cholesterol 103 mg
- Total Carbs 2.7 g
- Sugar 0.5 g
- Fiber 0.1 g
- Sodium 299 mg
- Potassium 109 mg
- Protein 5 g

Chocolate Cheese Cake

Preparation Time: 10 minutes
Cooking Time: 15 minutes
Servings: 6
Ingredients:
- 2 cups cream cheese, softened
- 2 eggs
- 2 tablespoons cocoa powder
- 1 teaspoon pure vanilla extract
- ½ cup swerve

Method:
1- Place eggs, cocoa powder, vanilla extract, swerve and cream cheese in an immersion blender and blend until smooth.
2- Pulse until well combined and transfer the mixture evenly into mason jars.
3- Put the mason jars in the insert of Ninja Foodi and lock the lid.
4- Press "Bake/Roast" and bake for about 15 minutes at 360 degrees F.
5- Refrigerate for at least 2 hours before serving and serve chilled.

Nutritional Value:
- Calories 244
- Total Fat 24.8 g
- Saturated Fat 15.6 g
- Cholesterol 32 mg
- Total Carbs 2.1 g
- Sugar 0.4 g
- Fiber 0.1 g
- Sodium 204 mg
- Potassium 81 mg
- Protein 4 g

Vanilla Yogurt

Preparation Time: 20 minutes
Cooking Time: 3 hours
Servings: 2
Ingredients:
- ½ cup full-fat milk
- ¼ cup yogurt starter
- 1 cup heavy cream
- ½ tablespoon pure vanilla extract
- 2 scoops stevia

Directions:
1. Pour milk in the pot of Ninja Foodi and stir in heavy cream, vanilla extract and stevia.
2. Allow the yogurt to sit and press "Slow Cooker" and cook on Low for about 3 hours.
3. Add the yogurt starter in 1 cup of milk and return this mixture to the pot.
4. Lock the lid and wrap the Ninja Foodi in two small towels.
5. Let sit for about 9 hours and allow the yogurt to culture.
6. Dish out in a serving bowl or refrigerate to serve.

Nutritional Value:
- Calories 292
- Total Fat 26.2 g
- Saturated Fat 16.3 g
- Cholesterol 100 mg
- Total Carbs 8.2 g
- Sugar 6.6 g
- Fiber 0 g
- Sodium 86 mg
- Potassium 250 mg
- Protein 5.2 g

Coffee Custard

Preparation Time: 20 minutes
Cooking Time: 10 minutes
Servings: 4
Ingredients:
- ounces mascarpone cream cheese
- 1 teaspoon espresso powder
- ¼ cup unsalted butter
- 4 large organic eggs, whites and yolks separated
- 1 tablespoon water
- ¼ teaspoon cream of tartar
- ½ teaspoon liquid stevia
- ¼ teaspoon monk fruit extract drops

Directions:
1. Press "Sauté" and "Lo:Md" on Ninja Foodi and add butter and cream cheese.
2. Sauté for about 3 minutes and stir in espresso powder, egg yolks and water.
3. Select "Lo" and cook for about for 4 minutes.
4. Meanwhile, whisk together egg whites, fruit drops, stevia and cream of tartar in a bowl.
5. Fold in the egg white mixture gently in the mixture in Ninja Foodi and cook for about 3 minutes.
6. Transfer it into serving glasses and refrigerate it for 3 hours before serving.

Nutritional Value:
- Calories 292
- Total Fat 26.2 g
- Saturated Fat 16.3 g
- Cholesterol 100 mg
- Total Carbs 8.2 g
- Sugar 6.6 g
- Fiber 0 g
- Sodium 86 mg
- Potassium 250 mg
- Protein 5.2 g

Fudge Divine

Preparation Time: 20 minutes
Cooking Time: 6 hours
Servings: 24
Ingredients:
- ½ teaspoon organic vanilla extract
- 1 cup heavy whipping cream
- 2-ounce butter, softened
- 2-ounce 70% dark chocolate, finely chopped

Directions:
1- Press "Sauté" and "Md:Hi" on Ninja Foodi and add vanilla and heavy cream.
2- Sauté for about 5 minutes and select "Lo".
3- Sauté for about 10 minutes and add butter and chocolate.
4- Sauté for about 2 minutes and transfer this mixture in a serving dish.
5- Refrigerate it for few hours and serve chilled.

Nutritional Value:
- Calories 292
- Total Fat 26.2 g
- Saturated Fat 16.3 g
- Cholesterol 100 mg
- Total Carbs 8.2 g
- Sugar 6.6 g
- Fiber 0 g
- Sodium 86 mg
- Potassium 250 mg
- Protein 5.2 g

Conclusion

The ketogenic diet has a vast array of medical benefits ranging from weight loss to treating various diseases like epilepsy. Lower intake of cabs makes the liver transform the fat in the body to fatty acids and ketonic bodies. These ketonic bodies are basically the fats and are used as the primary source of energy for the effective functioning of the body. The process of ketosis is initiated by the body as you start consuming a low carb intake in your diet. The ketogenic diet provides an atmosphere to the body to burn the already present and the fat intake in diet form for the functioning of the body instead of glucose.

The combo of both air frying and pressure cooking is the basic working principle of Ninja Foodi and is called the TenderCrisp Technology. It creates a perfect tender and juicy food which is crispy on its outer surface. The cooking procedures initiates with pressure cooking, followed by a customized air frying standard to achieve the crispiness of your choice. The Ninja Foodi is going to be a great help in establishing a perfect Keto lifestyle. The Ninja Foodi is going to make sure to provide you with the most delicious food to you and your loved ones in a little time and ensuring that your keto plan is always on without having any kind of hinderacnce. The Ninja Foodi can be used as any generally used cooking appliance and thus you can cook any keto food of your choice in no time.

Made in the USA
Columbia, SC
08 February 2019